Our Celebrations

Ellen Lawrence

LIGHTBOX
openlightbox.com

LIGHTBOX

Go to
www.openlightbox.com
and enter this book's
unique code.

ACCESS CODE

LBV96645

Lightbox is an all-inclusive digital solution for the teaching and learning of curriculum topics in an original, groundbreaking way. Lightbox is based on National Curriculum Standards.

OPTIMIZED FOR

- ✓ **TABLETS**
- ✓ **WHITEBOARDS**
- ✓ **COMPUTERS**
- ✓ **AND MUCH MORE!**

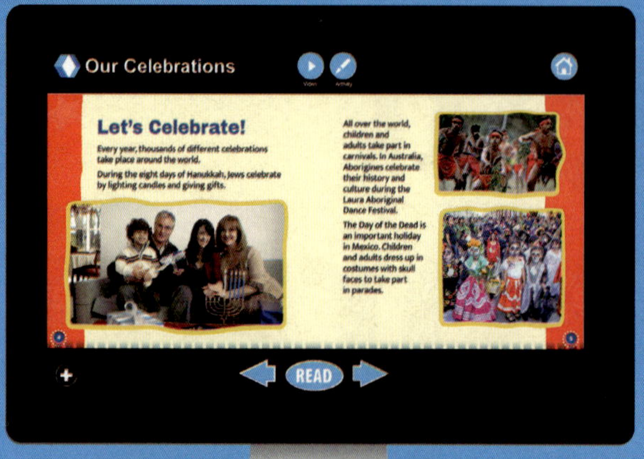

STANDARD FEATURES OF LIGHTBOX

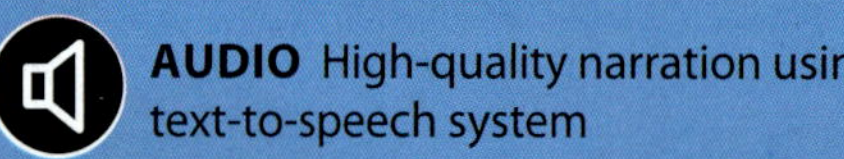
AUDIO High-quality narration using text-to-speech system

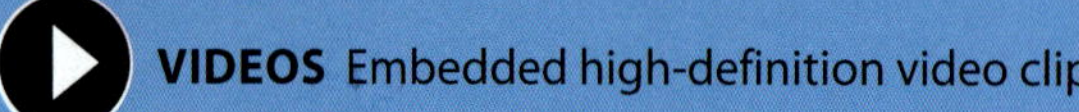
VIDEOS Embedded high-definition video clips

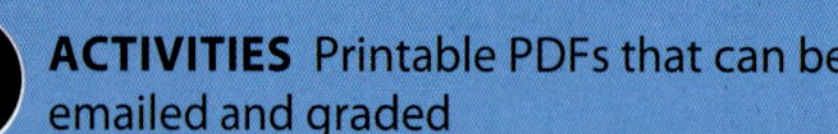
ACTIVITIES Printable PDFs that can be emailed and graded

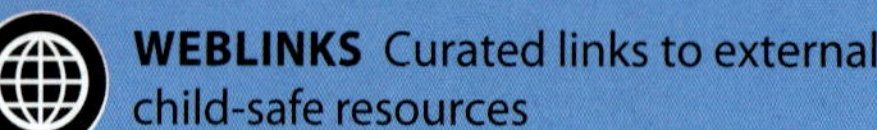
WEBLINKS Curated links to external, child-safe resources

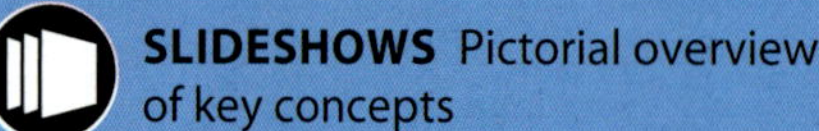
SLIDESHOWS Pictorial overviews of key concepts

INTERACTIVE MAPS Interactive maps and aerial satellite imagery

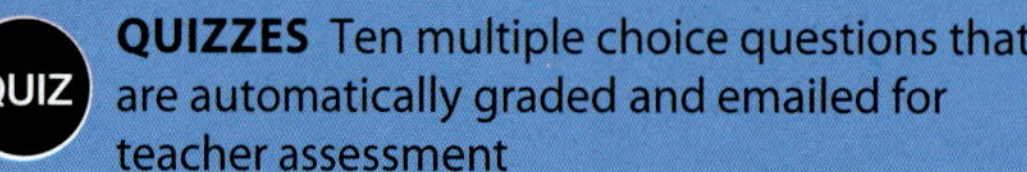
QUIZZES Ten multiple choice questions that are automatically graded and emailed for teacher assessment

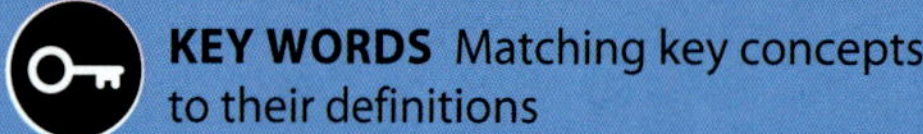
KEY WORDS Matching key concepts to their definitions

VIDEOS

WEBLINKS

SLIDESHOWS

QUIZZES

About Our World

Our Celebrations

Lightbox Access Code 2
Let's Celebrate! 4
A Viking Festival 6
Chinese New Year 8
The Festival of Holi 10
Cherry Blossom Time 12
Celebrating Eid al-Fitr 14
The Naadam Festival 16
The Cattle Crossing 18
Happy Thanksgiving! 20
What Have You Learned? 22
Key Words 24

Let's Celebrate!

Every year, thousands of different celebrations take place around the world.

During the eight days of Hanukkah, Jews celebrate by lighting candles and giving gifts.

All over the world, children and adults take part in carnivals. In Australia, Aborigines celebrate their history and culture during the Laura Aboriginal Dance Festival.

The Day of the Dead is an important holiday in Mexico. Children and adults dress up in costumes with skull faces to take part in parades.

A Viking Festival

In a town called Lerwick in the Shetland Islands, the new year begins with the Up Helly Aa festival.

About 1,000 years ago, these Scottish islands were home to Vikings. Up Helly Aa celebrates this history with parties and a parade.

Hundreds of people dressed as Vikings walk through the town carrying burning torches.

At the end of the parade, the Vikings march around a huge model of a Viking ship. Then they throw their torches onto the ship and set it on fire.

Chinese New Year

Chinese New Year is the most important holiday for Chinese people. It takes place in late January or early February.

More people live in Shanghai, China, than any other city in the world.

At New Year, people put the past behind them and celebrate new beginnings. They wear new clothes and clean their homes to sweep away bad luck. Families get together to enjoy large feasts and watch fireworks. Children receive gifts of small red envelopes that contain money.

New Year parades are held around the world in cities where Chinese people live. The parades include dancers carrying large, puppet-like dragons.

The Festival of Holi

In India, the arrival of spring is celebrated with the festival of Holi. It is also known as the festival of color.

On the night before Holi, people sing and dance. They roast chicken, coconut, and popcorn on bonfires.

The next day, everyone throws powdered paint and colored water at each other in the streets. Kids throw paint at adults, and it's even okay to throw paint at strangers!

Holi is a Hindu celebration. The custom of throwing colored paint comes from a story about the Hindu god Krishna. It is said that when Krishna was a little boy, he threw colored water over milkmaids who were milking cows.

Cherry Blossom Time

In Japan, people know that spring has arrived when pink and white blossoms appear on cherry trees. The blossoms last for just one or two weeks.

People gather in parks to see the cherry blossoms. They also hold outdoor parties. Families and friends have picnics under the trees as blossoms gently fall on them.

The Japanese custom of visiting parks and gardens to see and enjoy the cherry blossoms is called hanami. *Hanami* means "flower viewing." People in Japan have celebrated this time for hundreds of years.

Celebrating Eid al-Fitr

Ramadan is a very important month for Muslims. During daylight hours, adults and teenagers fast, or don't eat. People pray and try to give up bad habits.

Muslims celebrate the end of Ramadan with a big festival called Eid al-Fitr (EED ahl-FIT-ur).

On the first day of Eid al-Fitr, families and friends gather to eat a special daytime meal.

In many countries, Eid al-Fitr is celebrated over three days.

During Eid al-Fitr, people wear their best clothes and children receive gifts. People also give money to the poor. This money helps poor people buy food and new clothes. Then they can also enjoy the celebrations.

The Naadam Festival

Hooves thunder over the dusty grass. An excited crowd cheers on the horses and riders. It's midsummer in Mongolia and time for Naadam!

Naadam festivals, or games, are held throughout Mongolia. Each festival begins with a big parade. Then competitors take part in Mongolia's three favorite sports—wrestling, archery, and horse racing.

Some of the Naadam horse races are 17 miles (27 kilometers) long. All the jockeys, or riders, are children. Some of the riders are just five years old!

The Cattle Crossing

The Fulani people of Mali, in Africa, are cattle herders. For most of the year, many Fulani men live miles from home. They walk from place to place, finding grass for their animals.

In December, the herders and thousands of cattle return home by crossing the Niger River. The herders' families gather on the riverbank to welcome them home.

The time of the cattle crossing is a great celebration for Fulani families. Husbands, fathers, and older brothers have been gone for many months. Everyone celebrates with music, dancing, and feasting.

Happy Thanksgiving!

Every November, people all over the United States celebrate Thanksgiving. It's a time to get together with family and friends.

In 1621, the Pilgrims and their Native American neighbors shared a feast to celebrate a good harvest. Americans think of this as the first Thanksgiving.

Today, American families still enjoy a Thanksgiving feast of turkey, stuffing, cranberry sauce, sweet potatoes, and pumpkin pie.

Not everyone has a place to live or enough money to buy food for a Thanksgiving dinner. So every year, many people help out by cooking Thanksgiving dinners for people in need.

What are some of the reasons why people have celebrations?

How are celebrations done in the same way? How are they done differently?

KEY WORDS

Research has shown that as much as 65 percent of all written material published in English is made up of 300 words. These 300 words cannot be taught using pictures or learned by sounding them out. They must be recognized by sight. This book contains 123 common sight words to help young readers improve their reading fluency and comprehension. This book also teaches young readers several important content words, such as proper nouns. These words are paired with pictures to aid in learning and improve understanding.

Page	Sight Words First Appearance
4	and, around, by, different, every, of, place, take, the, world, years
5	all, an, children, day, important, in, is, over, part, their, to, up, with
6	a, about, home, new, these, this, were
7	as, at, end, it, on, people, set, then, they, through
8	any, city, for, live, more, most, or, other, than
9	are, away, get, large, like, put, small, that, them, together, watch, where
10	also, before, each, even, Indian, next, night, water
11	boy, from, he, little, said, story, was, when, who
12	has, just, know, last, one, time, trees, two, white
13	have, means, see, under
14	big, eat, first, give, many, three, try, very
15	can, food
17	long, miles, old, some
18	animals, men
19	fathers, been, great
20	American, family, good, states, think
21	enough, help, need, not, out, so, still

Page	Content Words First Appearance
4	candles, celebrations, gifts, Hanukkah, Jews
5	Aborigines, adults, Australia, carnivals, costumes, culture, Day of the Dead, faces, history, Mexico, parades
6	Lerwick, parties, Shetland Islands, town, Up Helly Aa, Vikings
7	fire, ship, torches
8	Chinese New Year, February, January, Shanghai
9	clothes, dragons, envelopes, feasts, fireworks, luck, money
10	bonfires, chicken, coconut, Holi, paint, popcorn, strangers
11	cows, Krishna, milkmaids
12	blossom, cherry, Japan, spring, weeks
13	hanami, gardens, parks, picnics
14	daylight, daytime, Eid al-Fitr, habits, meal, Muslims, Ramadan, teenagers
16	hooves, horses, Mongolia, Nandam, riders
17	archery, competitors, games, jockeys, racing, sports, wrestling
18	Africa, cattle, Fulani, grass, heroes, Mali
19	brothers, December, months, Niger River, music, riverbank
20	harvest, neighbors, November, pilgrims, Thanksgiving, United States
21	cranberry, pie, pumpkin, sauce, stuffing, sweet potatoes, turkey

Published by Smartbook Media Inc.
350 5th Avenue, 59th Floor New York, NY 10118
Website: www.openlightbox.com

Printed in the United States of America in Brainerd, Minnesota
1 2 3 4 5 6 7 8 9 0 22 21 20 19 18

012018
120117

Library of Congress Cataloging in Publication Control Number: 2017959799

ISBN 978-1-5105-3548-0 (hardcover)
ISBN 978-1-5105-3549-7 (multi-user eBook)

Project Coordinator: John Willis
Art Director: Terry Paulhus

Every reasonable effort has been made to trace ownership and to obtain permission to reprint copyright material. The publisher would be pleased to have any errors or omissions brought to its attention so that they may be corrected in subsequent printings.
The publisher acknowledges Getty Images and Alamy as its primary image suppliers for this title.